A VICTORIAN POSY

PENHALIGON'S
SCENTED TREASURY
OF VERSE AND
PROSE

A Victorian Posy

Edited by Sheila Pickles

LONDON MCMLXXXVII

For F. Z.

CONTENTS

Dear Reader,

My love of scent, of flowers and of poetry has meant that the selection of these floral passages has been a pleasure. I have tried to include some old favourites so there will be something familiar within these leaves for everyone. I have also been careful to include those whose attitudes embodied the Victorian spirit, such as Browning and Hardy, whilst excluding those with more contemporary attitudes, like Vita Sackville-West, even though she was born a Victorian.

I was surprised to find how many Victorian writers personified flowers as children or faeries, and I came to realise that flowers, like scent, are most evocative. They recall in my case the happiest of childhoods; long sunny days playing Hide and Seek in the herbaceous borders or

curled up in the hammock with a book. It is from my
parents that I have inherited a love of flowers, and the
piece written by Mrs. C. W. Earle about the Chrysanthemum Shows is included as a tribute to my father, whose
beloved blooms brought home prizes each year from the
local flower show but were equally difficult to arrange on
account of their size. It is from my grandmother that I
have inherited a love of poetry, and it is from her tiny
leather-bound poetry books that I made my choice. This
selection would not have been complete, however, without
a piece from *Tess of the d'Urbervilles*, a book read in class
at school, where we were taught with such enthusiasm that
my school-friends and I have retained our love for the
written word to the present day.

I would like to acknowledge my family, who were
largely ignored during the preparation of the book, those
friends who allowed me to raid their libraries, and the
creative team who helped me to put the book together.

I hope it will give you many hours of pleasure.

Sheila Pickles
Canonbury,
London

SPRING

" And in green underwood and cover
Blossom by blossom the spring begins "

ANOTHER SPRING

IF I might see another Spring,
   I'd not plant summer flowers and wait:
I'd have my crocuses at once,
My leafless pink mezereons,
   My chill-veined snowdrops, choicer yet
   My white or azure violet,
Leaf-nested primrose; anything
   To blow at once, not late.

If I might see another Spring,
   I'd listen to the daylight birds
That build their nests and pair and sing,
Nor wait for mateless nightingale;
   I'd listen to the lusty herds,
   The ewes with lambs as white as snow,
I'd find out music in the hail
   And all the winds that blow.

If I might see another Spring—
   Oh stinging comment on my past
That all my past results in "if"—
   If I might see another Spring
I'd laugh to-day, to-day is brief;
I would not wait for anything:
   I'd use to-day that cannot last,
   Be glad to-day and sing.

CHRISTINA ROSSETTI, 1830-1894

Now a few yards farther, and I reach the bank. Ah! I smell them already— their exquisite perfume steams and lingers in this moist, heavy air. Through this little gate, and along the green south bank of this green wheat-field, and they burst upon me, the lovely violets, in tenfold loveliness. The ground is covered with them, white and purple, enamelling the short dewy grass, looking but the more vividly coloured under the dull, leaden sky. There they lie by hundreds, by thousands. In former years I have been used to watch them from the tiny green bud, till one or two stole into bloom. They never came on me before in such a sudden and luxuriant glory of simple beauty,—and I do really owe one pure and genuine pleasure to feverish London! How beautifully they are placed too, on this sloping bank, with the palm branches waving over them, full of early bees, and mixing their honeyed scent with the more delicate violet odour! How transparent and smooth and lusty are the branches, full of sap and life! And there, just by the old mossy root, is a superb tuft of primroses, with a yellow butterfly hovering over them, like a flower floating on the air. What happiness to sit on this tufty knoll, and fill my basket with the blossoms! What a renewal of heart and mind!

OUR VILLAGE, MARY RUSSELL MITFORD, 1787-1855

SONG

Hail! fairy queen, adorned with flowers,
Attended by the smiling hours,
'Tis thine to dress the rosy bowers
   In colours gay;
We love to wander in thy train,
To meet thee on the fertile plain
To bless thy soft propitious reign,
   O lovely May!

'Tis thine to dress the vale anew,
In fairest verdure bright with dew;
And harebells of the mildest blue,
   Smile in thy way;
Then let us welcome pleasant spring,
And still the flowery tribute bring,
And still to thee our carol sing,
   O lovely May!

Now by the genial zephyr fanned,
The blossoms of the rose expand;
And reared by thee with gentle hand,
   Their charms display;
The air is balmy and serene,
And all the sweet luxuriant scene
By thee is clad in tender green,
   O lovely May!

MRS. HEMANS, 1793-1835

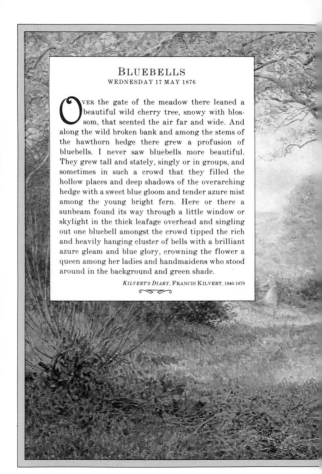

BLUEBELLS
WEDNESDAY 17 MAY 1876

OVER the gate of the meadow there leaned a beautiful wild cherry tree, snowy with blossom, that scented the air far and wide. And along the wild broken bank and among the stems of the hawthorn hedge there grew a profusion of bluebells. I never saw bluebells more beautiful. They grew tall and stately, singly or in groups, and sometimes in such a crowd that they filled the hollow places and deep shadows of the overarching hedge with a sweet blue gloom and tender azure mist among the young bright fern. Here or there a sunbeam found its way through a little window or skylight in the thick leafage overhead and singling out one bluebell amongst the crowd tipped the rich and heavily hanging cluster of bells with a brilliant azure gleam and blue glory, crowning the flower a queen among her ladies and handmaidens who stood around in the background and green shade.

KILVERT'S DIARY, FRANCIS KILVERT, 1840–1879

THE RHODORA
ON BEING ASKED, WHENCE IS THE FLOWER?

IN MAY, when sea-winds pierced our solitudes,
I found the fresh Rhodora in the woods,
Spreading its leafless blooms in a damp nook,
To please the desert and the sluggish brook.
The purple petals, fallen in the pool,
Made the black water with their beauty gay;
Here might the red-bird come his plumes to cool,
And court the flower that cheapens his array.
Rhodora! if the sages ask thee why
This charm is wasted on the earth and sky,
Tell them, dear, that if eyes were made for seeing,
Then Beauty is its own excuse for being:
Why thou wert there, O rival of the rose!
I never thought to ask, I never knew;
But, in my simple ignorance, suppose
The self-same Power that brought me there brought you.

RALPH WALDO EMERSON, 1803-1882

PUSSY-WILLOWS

B<small>Y</small> the road-side, in the field,
    Greeting each new-comer,—
Pussy-willows wave their plumes,
    Heralding the summer.

A<small>NON</small>

SUMMER

" A thousand flowers – each seeming one
That learnt by gazing at the sun."

❧ IRREPARABLENESS ❧

I HAVE been in the meadows all the day,
And gathered there the nosegay that you see,
Singing within myself as bird or bee
When such do field-work on a morn of May.
But now I look upon my flowers, decay
Has met them in my hands, more fatally
Because more warmly clasped,—and sobs are free
To come instead of songs. What you say,
Sweet counsellors, dear friends? that I should go
Back straightway to the fields and gather more?
Another, sooth, may do it, but not I.
My heart is very tired, my strength is low,
My hands are full of blossoms plucked before,
Held dead within them till myself shall die.

ELIZABETH BARRETT BROWNING. 1806-1861

A YELLOW PANSY

TO THE wall of the old green garden
    A butterfly quivering came;
His wings on the sombre lichens
    Played like a yellow flame.

He looked at the grey geraniums,
    And the sleepy four-o'clocks;
He looked at the low lanes bordered
    With the glossy-growing box.

He longed for the peace and the silence,
    And the shadows that lengthened there,
And his wee wild heart was weary
    Of skimming the endless air.

And now in the old green garden,—
    I know not how it came,—
A single pansy is blooming,
    Bright as a yellow flame.

And whenever a gay gust passes,
    It quivers as if with pain,
For the butterfly-soul that is in it
    Longs for the winds again!

HELEN GRAY CONE, 19th CENTURY

THE POPPIES IN THE GARDEN

THE poppies in the garden, they all wear frocks of silk,
Some are purple, some are pink, and others white as milk,
Light, light, for dancing in, for dancing when the breeze
Plays a little two-step for the blossoms and the bees.
Fine, fine, for dancing in, all frilly at the hem,
Oh, when I watch the poppies dance I long to dance like them!

The poppies in the garden have let their silk frocks fall
All about the border paths, but where are they at all?
Here a frill and there a flounce—a rag of silky red,
But not a poppy-girl is left—I think they've gone to bed.
Gone to bed and gone to sleep; and weary they must be,
For each has left her box of dreams upon the stem for me.

FFRIDA WOLFE, 19th CENTURY

WOMEN AND ROSES

I DREAM of a red-rose tree.
And which of its roses three
Is the dearest rose to me?

Round and round, like a dance of snow
In a dazzling drift, as its guardians, go
Floating the women faded for ages,
Sculptured in stone, on the poet's pages.
Then follow women fresh and gay,
Living and loving and loved to-day.
Last, in the rear, flee the multitude of maidens,
Beauties yet unborn. And all, to one cadence,
They circle their rose on my rose tree.

ROBERT BROWNING. 1812-1889

THERE IS NOTHING HELD SO DEAR

THERE is nothing held so dear
  As love, if only it be hard to win.
The roses that in yonder hedge appear
  Outdo our garden-buds which bloom within;
But since the hand may pluck them every day,
Unmarked they bud, bloom, drop, and drift away.

JEAN INGELOW, 1820-1897

Tess went down the hill to Trantridge Cross, and inattentively waited to take her seat in the van returning from Chaseborough to Shaston. She did not know what the other occupants said to her as she entered, though she answered them; and when they had started anew she rode along with an inward and not an outward eye.

One among her fellow-travellers addressed her more pointedly than any had spoken before: "Why, you be quite a posy! And such roses in early June!"

Then she became aware of the spectacle she presented to their surprised vision: roses at her breast; roses in her hat; roses and strawberries in her basket to the brim. She blushed, and said confusedly that the flowers had been given to her. When the passengers were not looking she stealthily removed the more prominent blooms from her hat and placed them in the basket, where she covered them with her handkerchief. Then she fell to reflecting again, and in looking downwards a thorn of the rose remaining in her breast accidentally pricked her chin. Like all the cottagers in Blackmoor Vale, Tess was steeped in fancies and prefigurative superstitions; she thought this an ill omen—the first she had noticed that day.

TESS OF THE D'URBERVILLES
THOMAS HARDY, 1840-1928

THE HONEYSUCKLE

I PLUCKED a honeysuckle where
   The hedge on high is quick with thorn,
   And climbing for the prize, was torn,
And fouled my feet in quag-water;
   And by the thorns and by the wind
   The blossom that I took was thinn'd,
And yet I found it sweet and fair.

Thence to a richer growth I came,
   Where, nursed in mellow intercourse,
   The honeysuckles sprang by scores,
Not harried like my single stem,
   All virgin lamps of scent and dew.
   So from my hand that first I threw,
Yet plucked not any more of them.

DANTE GABRIEL ROSSETTI 1828-1882

THE DANDELION

WITH locks of gold to-day;
To-morrow, silver grey;
Then blossom-bald. Behold,
O man, thy fortune told!

JOHN B. TABB. 19th CENTURY

THE GARDENER

THE gardener does not love to talk,
  He makes me keep the gravel walk;
And when he puts his tools away,
He locks the door and takes the key.

Away behind the currant row
Where no one else but cook may go,
Far in the plots, I see him dig,
Old and serious, brown and big.

He digs the flowers, green, red, and blue,
Nor wishes to be spoken to.
He digs the flowers and cuts the hay,
And never seems to want to play.

Silly gardener! summer goes,
And winter comes with pinching toes,
When in the garden bare and brown
You must lay your barrow down.

Well now, and while the summer stays,
To profit by these garden days,
O how much wiser you would be
To play at Indian wars with me!

ROBERT LOUIS STEVENSON, 1850-1894

"TIGER-LILY!" said Alice, addressing herself to one that was waving gracefully about in the wind, "I *wish* you could talk!"

"We *can* talk," said the Tiger-lily, "when there's anybody worth talking to."

Alice was so astonished that she couldn't speak for a minute: it quite seemed to take her breath away. At length, as the Tiger-lily only went on waving about, she spoke again, in a timid voice—almost in a whisper. "And can *all* the flowers talk?"

"As well as you can," said the Tiger-lily. "And a great deal louder."

"It isn't manners for us to begin, you know," said the Rose, "and I really was wondering when you'd speak! Said I to myself, 'Her face has got *some* sense in it, though it's not a clever one!' Still, you're the right colour, and that goes a long way."

"I don't care about the colour," the Tiger-lily remarked. "If only her petals curled up a little more, she'd be all right."

Alice didn't like being criticized, so she began asking questions. "Aren't you sometimes frightened at being planted out here, with nobody to take care of you?"

"There's the tree in the middle," said the Rose. "What else is it good for?"

"But what could it do, if any danger came?" Alice asked.

"It could bark," said the Rose.

"It says 'Bough-wough!'" cried a Daisy. "That's why its branches are called boughs!"

"Didn't you know *that*?" cried another Daisy. And here they all began shouting together, till the air seemed quite full of little shrill voices.

"Silence, every one of you!" cried the Tiger-lily, waving itself passionately from side to side, and trembling with excitement. "They know I can't get at them!" it panted, bending its quivering head towards Alice, "or they wouldn't dare to do it!"

"Never mind!" Alice said in a soothing tone, and, stooping down to the Daisies, who were just beginning again, she whispered "If you don't hold your tongues, I'll pick you!"

There was silence in a moment, and several of the pink Daisies turned white.

"That's right!" said the Tiger-lily. "The Daisies are worst of all. When one speaks, they all begin together, and it's enough to make one wither to hear the way they go on!"

"How is it you can all talk so nicely?" Alice said, hoping to get it into a better temper by a compliment. "I've been in many gardens before, but none of the flowers could talk."

"Put your hand down, and feel the ground," said the Tiger-lily. "Then you'll know why."

Alice did so. "It's very hard," she said; "but I don't see what that has to do with it."

"In most gardens," the Tiger-lily said, "they make the beds too soft—so that the flowers are always asleep."

This sounded a very good reason, and Alice was quite pleased to know it. "I never thought of that before!" she said.

"It's my opinion that you never think *at all*," the Rose said, in a rather severe tone.

"I never saw anybody that looked stupider," a Violet said, so suddenly that Alice quite jumped; for it hadn't spoken before.

"Hold *your* tongue!" cried the Tiger-lily. "As if *you* ever saw anybody! You keep your head under the leaves, and snore away there, till you know no more what's going on in the world, than if you were a bud!"

LEWIS CARROLL, 1832-1898

AUTUMN

" And frosts and shortening days portend
The aged year is near his end. "

FRINGED GENTIAN

GOD made a little gentian;
　It tried to be a rose
And failed, and all the summer laughed.
　But just before the snows
There came a purple creature
　That ravished all the hill;
And summer hid her forehead,
　And mockery was still.
The frosts were her condition;
　The Tyrian would not come
Until the North evoked it,
　"Creator! shall I bloom?"

EMILY DICKINSON, 1830-1886

THE SEA-POPPY

A POPPY grows upon the shore,
Bursts her twin cup in summer late:
Her leaves are glaucous-green and hoar,
Her petals yellow, delicate.

Oft to her cousins turns her thought,
In wonder if they care that she
Is fed with spray for dew, and caught
By every gale that sweeps the sea.

She has no lovers like the red,
That dances with the noble corn:
Her blossoms on the waves are shed,
Where she stands shivering and forlorn.

ROBERT BRIDGES, 1844-1930

IN THE WOOD

IN THE wood where shadows are deepest
From the branches overhead,
Where the wild wood-strawberries cluster,
And the softest moss is spread,
I met today with a fairy,
And I followed her where she led.

Some magical words she uttered,
I alone could understand,
For the sky grew bluer and brighter;
While there rose on either hand
The cloudy walls of a palace
That was built in Fairy-land.

And I stood in a strange enchantment;
I had known it all before:
In my heart of hearts was the magic
Of days that will come no more,
The magic of joy departed,
That Time can never restore.

That never, ah, never, never,
Never again can be: —
Shall I tell you what powerful fairy
Built up this palace for me?
It was only a little white violet
I found at the root of a tree.

ADELAIDE A. PROCTER, 1825-1864

OCTOBER

I ALWAYS long at this time of the year to have been to Japan to see one of their Chrysanthemum shows. I am told our individual flowers are far finer, but their method of arranging the shows is so superior to ours, and the effect produced is naturally much more lovely. They arrange them in bands and waves of colour, from the darkest red to the palest pink, fading into white; and up again from pale lemon, yellow, and orange to the darkest brown. I am sure, even in small collections, picked and unpicked Chrysanthemums look far better if the colours are kept together in clumps, and not dotted about till the general effect becomes mud-colour, as English gardeners always arrange them, only considering their height or the size of their unnaturally disbudded blooms. They are, I admit, most beautiful and useful flowers. What should we do without them? But owners of small places, and I think even large ones, should guard against too much time, attention, and room being given to them. For putting into vases, there is no doubt Chrysanthemums look better allowed to grow more naturally and not so disbudded. A huge Chrysanthemum that is nearly the size of a plate, though it may have won a prize at a local flower-show, looks almost vulgar when picked. Bunches of Chrysanthemums with their buds will go on blooming a long time in water, and make in a room a natural and beautiful decoration, instead of painfully reminding one of the correctness of the flower's paper imitations.

POT-POURRI FROM A SURREY GARDEN, MRS. C. W. EARLE, 1836-1925

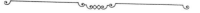

❧ TABLE DECORATION ☙

FLOWERS FOR DECORATION should be those which are not very strongly scented. To some the perfume of such flowers as gardenias, stephanotis, hyacinths and others is not offensive, but to others the strong scent in a heated room, especially during dinner, is considered very unpleasant. Otherwise, there is no dictating what the flowers should be. It is well to avoid many colours in one decoration, for, even if well grouped, they are seldom as effective as one or two mixed with white and green. It is a fashion to have a single colour for a dinner-table decoration, this being often chosen of the same tint as the hostess's dress or the hangings of the room, though these are sometimes varied to suit the flowers. Again, all white flowers are very often employed, relieved by plenty of foliage.

MRS. BEETON, 1836-1865

WINTER

"The winter comes: the frozen rut
Is bound with silver bars."

⟿❖ THE SEASONS ❖⟿

THEN sleep the seasons, full of might;
  While slowly swells the pod,
And rounds the peach, and in the night
  The mushroom bursts the sod.

The winter comes: the frozen rut
  Is bound with silver bars;
The white drift heaps against the hut;
  And night is pierced with stars.

COVENTRY PATMORE, 1823-1896

EARTH has borne a little son ;
    He is a very little one.
He has a head of golden hair
And a grave unwinking stare.
He wears a bib all frilled and green
Round his neck to keep him clean.
Though before another spring
A thousand children Earth may bring
Forth to bid a blossoming—
Lily daughters, cool and slender,
Roses passionate and tender,
Tulip sons as brave as swords,
Hollyhocks like laughing lords—
Yet she 'll never love them quite
As much as she loves Aconite—
Aconite, the first of all,
Who is so very, very small ;
Who is so golden-haired and good,
And wears a bib as babies should.

ANON

OUTSIDE

KING Winter sat in his Hall one day,
   And he said to himself, said he,
"I must admit I've had some fun,
I've chilled the Earth and cooled the Sun,
   And not a flower or tree
But wishes that my reign were done,
And as long as Time and Tide shall run,
I'll go on making everyone
   As cold as cold can be."

There came a knock at the outer door :
   "Who's there?" King Winter cried ;
"Open your Palace Gate," said Spring
"For you can reign no more as King,
   Nor longer here abide ;
This message from the Sun I bring,
'The trees are green, the birds do sing ;
The hills with joy are echoing':
   So pray, Sir—step outside !"

HUGH CHESTERMAN, 19th CENTURY

"Stay a little longer," said the children to
  the snowdrop,
  "Stay a little longer by the old laburnum tree."
But she said, "I must be going,
Be it hailing, raining, snowing,
I must stir me and be going
For the Master calleth me."

"Stay a little longer," said the children to
   the snowdrop,
"Stay a little longer in your nut-brown nursery."
But she said, "I must be homing
To my sisters in the gloaming,
I must stir me and be homing
For the Master calleth me."

ANON

❧ Flower Chorus ❧

Such a commotion under the ground,
　　When March called, "Ho there! ho!"
Such spreading of rootlets far and wide,
　　Such whisperings to and fro!
"Are you ready?" the Snowdrop asked,
　　" 'Tis time to start, you know."
"Almost, my dear!" the Scilla replied,
　　"I'll follow as soon as you go."
Then "Ha! ha! ha!" a chorus came
　　Of laughter sweet and low,
From millions of flowers under the ground,
　　Yes, millions beginning to grow.

"I'll promise my blossoms," the Crocus said,
　　"When I hear the blackbird sing."
And straight thereafter Narcissus cried,
　　"My silver and gold I'll bring."
"And ere they are dulled," another spoke,
　　"The Hyacinth bells shall ring."
But the Violet only murmured, "I'm here,"
　　And sweet grew the air of Spring.

O the pretty brave things, thro' the coldest days
　　Imprisoned in walls of brown,
They never lost heart tho' the blast shrieked loud,
　　And the sleet and the hail came down;
But patiently each wrought her wonderful dress,
　　Or fashioned her beautiful crown,
And now they are coming to lighten the world
　　Still shadowed by winter's frown.
And well may they cheerily laugh "Ha! ha!"
　　In laughter sweet and low,
The millions of flowers under the ground,
　　Yes, millions beginning to grow.

RALPH W. EMERSON. 1803-1882

PICTURE ACKNOWLEDGEMENTS

The majority of the illustrations were supplied by Fine Art Photographic Library, London unless otherwise indicated.

In order of appearance
J O Banks ; Johann Laurents Jensen ; Joseph Kirkpatrick ; Christine Marie Loumand ; Henry J Johnstone ; Edwin Steele ; Myles Birkett Foster ; Charles Gregory (Bourne Gallery) ; James Hayllar ; George Dunlop Leslie ; Noel Smith ; Henry Wallis ; Edmund Julius Detmold ; John H Dell ; Edward Killingworth Johnson ; Eva Hollyer ; Edward Killingworth Johnson ; Vincent Clare ; Henry Ryland ; Sophie Anderson ; William Stephen Coleman, Limpsfield Watercolours ; William Scott Myles ; Anthony Mitchell Paintings ; Mary Hayllar ; From *Mrs Loudon's Flower Garden*, Royal Horticultural Society ; Edward Wilkins Wait ; Thomas Creswick ; Edward Wilkins Wait ; From *Mrs Loudon's Flower Garden*, Royal Horticultural Society ; From *Mrs Loudon's Flower Garden*, Royal Horticultural Society ; Richard Doyle, British Museum Prints and Drawings ; Tenniel from *Alice Through the Looking Glass* ; Marianne North, HMSO, Royal Botanic Gardens, Kew ; From *Mrs Beeton's Book of Household Management* ; John Ritchie ; Edward Wilkins Waite ; From *Mrs Loudon's Flower Garden*, Royal Horticultural Society ; Anon, Nister's Annual ; R Drew ; Mary Ensor, Christopher Wood Gallery. Jacket : *Jour A Droite* by Henry Wallis.

PENHALIGON'S

In 1975 Franco Zeffirelli suggested to me that I might like to take over the dying business of Penhaligon's, the perfumery which had been founded a little over a 100 years earlier. By doing so he opened up a whole new world for me. A world of magical scents, mysterious potions, and limitless possibilities. In developing the business, I have tried to live up to the high standard set by its founder William Henry Penhaligon, who left a valuable portfolio of formulae on which to base new perfumes. One of these, Victorian Posy, was created as a result of a request from Dr. Roy Strong, who was planning an exhibition entitled "The Garden" for the Victoria and Albert Museum in 1979 and invited Penhaligon's to celebrate the exhibition by reserving one of our scents for the occasion. I therefore developed Victorian Posy as the most English of scents, for it contains only English country garden flowers, and has the scent of a true Victorian Posy.

Following its success, it seemed natural to complement Victorian Posy by the addition of a book, sweetly scented and reflecting the floral theme.

Sheila Pickles

Published in the United States by Harmony Books, a
division of Crown Publishers, Inc., 201 East 50th Street,
New York, New York, 10022. Member of the Crown
Publishing Group.

Published in Great Britain by Pavilion Books Limited

Random House, Inc. New York, Toronto, London, Sydney,
Auckland

HARMONY and colphon are trademarks of Crown Publishers,
Inc.

Manufactured in Singapore

Design by Bernard Higton

Library of Congress Catalog Card Number: 87-61525

ISBN 0-517-59901-5

10 9 8 7 6 5 4 3 2 1

First Miniature American Edition